WELCOME TO THE CONSTRUCTION SITE

Blasthole Drill

Samantha Bell

Published in the United States of America
by Cherry Lake Publishing
Ann Arbor, Michigan
www.cherrylakepublishing.com

Content Adviser: Louis Teel, Professor of Heavy Equipment Operating,
Central Arizona College
Reading Adviser: Cecilia Minden, PhD, Literacy expert and children's author

Photo Credits: ©xtrekx / Shutterstock, cover, 2; ©ledokolua / Shutterstock, 4;
©Massis / Shutterstock, 6; ©Ekalunda / Shutterstock 8; ©Dr Ajay Kumar Singh
/ Shutterstock, 10; ©Vladimir Melnik / Shutterstock, 12; ©Dmitri Melnik /
Shutterstock, 14; ©Gena Melendrez / Shutterstock, 16; ©iurii / Shutterstock,
18; ©Maksim Nazemtcev / Shutterstock, 20

Library of Congress Cataloging-in-Publication Data
Names: Bell, Samantha, author.
Title: Blasthole drill / by Samantha Bell.
Description: Ann Arbor : Cherry Lake Publishing, [2018] | Series: Welcome to
  the construction site | Includes bibliographical references and index. |
  Audience: Grades K to 3.
Identifiers: LCCN 2018003282| ISBN 9781534129245 (hardcover) | ISBN
  9781534132443 (pbk.) | ISBN 9781534130944 (pdf) | ISBN 9781534134140
  (hosted ebook)
Subjects: LCSH: Rock-drills—Juvenile literature. | Blasting
  machines—Juvenile literature. | Boring—Juvenile literature.
Classification: LCC TA745 .B45 2018 | DDC 624.1/526—dc23
LC record available at https://lccn.loc.gov/2018003282

Cherry Lake Publishing would like to acknowledge the work of The Partnership
for 21st Century Learning. Please visit www.p21.org for more information.

Printed in the United States of America
Corporate Graphics

Table of Contents

Breaking It Up

Blasthole **drills** make holes in rock. They help break the rock apart.

First, workers study the rock. They decide where a hole should go. Then they put the drill in place.

Motors and Bits

The drill has a sharp **bit**.
A machine turns the bit.

The bit makes a deep hole in the rock.

Why do workers need explosives?

A worker puts **explosives** in the hole.

Fire in the Hole!

The explosives are blown up. The rock breaks into pieces. Now it can be moved.

Blasthole drills help make way for roads. They help make **trenches** for pipes.

What can you find in a mine?

Roads, Trenches, Mines

Many drills are used in mines.

Blasthole drills help move rock out of the way!

Find Out More

Book

Sandvik—Multi-Function Drilling Rig

http://www.directindustry.com/prod/sandvik-mining-rock
-technology/product-40142-431512.html

Follow the link to watch how a blasthole drill works.

Website

Atlas Copco—Down-the-Hole Drilling Tools

www.atlascopco.com/en-us/mrba/products/rock-drilling-tools
/down-the-hole-drilling-tools

Learn more about what the tools made by this company do.

Glossary

bit (BIT) the pointed part of a drill that makes holes

drills (DRILZ) tools with a pointed end for making holes

explosives (ik-SPLOH-sivz) things that can blow up, such as
dynamite

mines (MYNZ) holes in the ground made for digging out things
like gold or coal

trenches (TRENCH-iz) long, narrow holes in the ground

Home and School Connection

Use this list of words from the book to help your child become a better reader. Word games and writing activities can help beginning readers reinforce literacy skills.

a	for	out	turns
apart	go	pieces	up
are	has	pipes	used
be	help	place	way
bit	hole	put	where
blasthole	in	puts	worker
blown	into	roads	workers
break	it	rock	
can	make	sharp	
decide	makes	should	
deep	mines	study	
drill	moved	the	
drills	now	they	
explosives	of	trenches	

Index

About the Author

Samantha Bell has written and illustrated over 60 books for children. She lives in South Carolina with her family and pets.

For my mom, who always supported and encouraged
my imagination and dreams ~ Karen Kilpatrick

For Summer & Jacob ~Tara Louise Campbell

Designed by KAREN KILPATRICK.

Nina Charles
Publishing

9924 NW 65 Manor, Parkland, Florida 33076

ISBN: 978-1-938447-19-8 Hardcover
ISBN: 978-1-938447-15-0 Softcover

Printed in China.

www.pumpkinheads.com

Publisher's Cataloging-In-Publication Data
(Prepared by The Donohue Group, Inc.)

Kilpatrick, Karen.
  Imagine / written by Karen Kilpatrick ; illustrated by Tara Louise Campbell & Matthew Wilson.

  pages : color illustrations ; cm. -- ([Pumpkinheads: learning through play])

  Summary: Slide down rainbows and swing from stars! Bounce on clouds and drive fast cars! Join
the Pumpkinheads as they switch the world around in a silly adventure that explores the power of
imagination and the differences that make the world beautiful. Includes extended learning activities.
  Interest age level: 004-008.
  ISBN: 978-1-938447-19-8

  1. Imagination--Juvenile fiction. 2. Individual differences--Juvenile fiction. 3. Imagination--Fiction.
4. Individuality--Fiction. 5. Stories in rhyme. I. Campbell, Tara Louise II. Wilson, Matthew, 1974- III.
Title.

PZ7.K556 Im 2015
[E]

2015932125

Imagine

Written by Karen Kilpatrick

Illustrated by Tara Louise Campbell & Matthew Wilson

Nina Charles Publishing

Parkland, Florida